Grandmas

LYNETTE HAYNES

Archway Publishing books may be ordered through booksellers or by contacting:

Archway Publishing
1663 Liberty Drive
Bloomington, IN 47403
www.archwaypublishing.com
844-669-3957

ISBN: 978-1-6657-2574-3 (sc)
ISBN: 978-1-6657-2572-9 (hc)
ISBN: 978-1-6657-2573-6 (e)

Print information available on the last page.

Archway Publishing rev. date: 2/2/2023

Grandmas

Grandmas are special women and may be young or old. More important, grandmas love their grandchildren and chat about them with pride.

Grandmas may be multilingual and speak different languages. What language does your grandma speak?

Grandmas have special names,
like *Granny, Bibi, Nana, GranGran,
Abuela,* and *Nai Nai.* What is
your grandma's special name?

Grandmas are wise and strong.
Sometimes they share advice and
help us solve life's problems.

Grandmas love to tell stories. They share old family tales and special stories of things that happened in their lives.

11

Grandmas love to cook and share favorite family recipes. What do you like to eat at grandma's place?

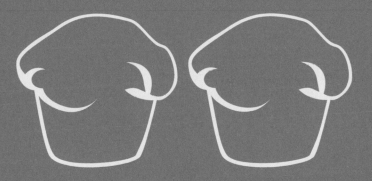

TRAVEL AIRWAYS
BARBADOS

GATE
5

Grandmas love to go on trips to learn more about the world. They may travel by car, plane, bus, train, or ship to interesting places. Sometimes they may even take along their grandchildren.

Grandmas love to work in the garden.
They take care of their gardens by
planting seeds, pruning branches,
pulling weeds, and watering plants.

Grandmas love to sing or dance. Some even like to play musical instruments such as the guitar, piano, violin or drums.

Grandmas love to spoil their grandchildren with lots of hugs and gifts for birthdays and holidays.

Some grandmas live far away from their families and keep in touch by sharing photos, writing letters, or talking on the phone to their grandchildren.

Photo of your Grandma

Photo of your Grandma

Name

Name

Most of all grandmas love to have fun and many grandchildren have two grandmas to enjoy!

Place a photo of each of your grandmas inside the blank boxes and write their special name under the picture.

About the Author

Lynette Haynes is retired, a mother of two, and a grandmother of three. She holds fond memories of her grandmother, a short, spunky, one-legged woman who told fascinating and inspiring stories.

Printed in the United States
by Baker & Taylor Publisher Services